LATE
WINTER SUN

SEEING LIFE DIFFERENTLY

The Poetry and Musings of
Alan Drummond Reid

Published by:

FriesenPress
Suite 300 – 852 Fort Street
Victoria, BC, Canada V8W 1H8

www.friesenpress.com

Distributed to the trade by The Ingram Book Company

Table of Contents

INTRODUCTION

Do you have plans for your retirement?" I was asked this question many times after announcing my retirement to family, friends and colleagues in early 2011. I suppose it was a normal question for people to ask, after extending their congratulations. I contented myself with responding that I had worked steadily for 45 years, and now that I was approaching my 70th year I deserved to withdraw from the active work force. I had paid my dues and would now set about the task of reinventing and reapplying myself.

Of course in today's world retirement has lost much of its significance, both legal and practical. Many working people have occupations and vocations that simply do not support it. How many people have I heard say: "I could never retire!" or "I will never retire!"? I had said that myself, many times, in my younger days, when I felt immortal and the thought of retirement made no sense to me. That was when retirement was the normal course – it was a social and legal institution that I was eager to rebel against. But somehow, having grown up in that age, the subliminal message must have been implanted. I watched my parents retire; I had friends who retired early and sang its praises; and about ten years ago I found myself beginning to focus on such essentials as pensions, savings and investments, the importance of which I had ignored for so many years.

Even so, retirement had been a bold step to take. I was reasonably happy in my work, and still quite good at it. I had eased into retirement by semi-retiring about a year and a half earlier, but even that was not enough to cushion the abruptness of clearing out my office and walking out the door for the last time on my retirement day. Metaphorically speaking, it was like walking into another world. I had the strong sense that nothing would look quite the same again. While I recognize that at this late stage of our lives the world actually does look very different than it did when we were younger, retirement seems to accentuate this by removing distractions and blinders with which work routinely shackles us. It is like removing a pair of dark glasses and realizing that they don't work that well once daylight has surrendered to the shadows of evening. It allows for what I think of as "retired eyes."

Hence the subtitle for this collection, *Seeing Life Differently*. Interestingly, years ago, in the early 1990s, it had been suggested to me that I write a book bearing that very title. At the time I had just published a book about the legal profession, as seen from my then newly acquired spiritual viewpoint, entitled *Seeing Law Differently*. As the book had been modestly successful, within a narrow reader audience, and as writing the book had greatly assisted me to carry on within that profession for another 20 years or so, it dawned on me that perhaps another therapeutic writing journey might be just what the doctor ordered to usher me into this new stage of life.

And so I began this literary journey by looking back on everything I had learned and experienced over my lifetime, in an effort to sort out what was still valuable, and what was not. My professional training, once my life blood, seemed to have lost much of its lustre, except for the occasional consulting, *pro bono* assistance and mentoring that I continued to offer. However, my academic training was definitely still useful: reading, writing, analysis and comprehension would be handy tools in this new venture I was considering. As I got deeper into my reflections, I realized that I had a passion to understand what this life is about, and a desire to leave traces of that understanding behind me for my children, and perhaps others, to ponder.

In taking stock of lessons I had learned thus far in life, several themes emerged, which I began to explore in preparation for my journey. At the top of my list, I discovered, was the importance of treating others with kindness and respect. This lesson is at the foundation of credible contemporary religions and spiritual belief systems, and separates us humans from the animal world, where survival appears to be the dominant order and driving force. Although not always readily apparent, the lesson can, with reasonable diligence, be found in our educational systems, legal systems, medicine, religion, the human sciences, and in most other institutional structures in contemporary society. However, it is often overshadowed by emphasis on rules, politics, theories, philosophies, dogmas and other influences. These, I feel, have often served to obscure, ignore, distort and misinterpret the lesson, with great human and environmental sacrifice. Countless examples are reported daily in news stories, have been recorded in history books, and populate our own personal experiences. People, in so many walks of life, have simply lost sight of the importance of treating one another with kindness and respect.

I believe that if there is meaning or purpose to our life's journey, it is to see through the layers that have clouded the core lesson just referred to, and others that flow from it, and to live life as consistently as possible with their messages. If we aspire to lofty objectives such as world peace, love, charity, compassion and equality, it falls to each of us to practice them. If we want world peace, we can practice peace in our immediate and extended world. If we want to experience love in our lives, we can practice love in our relationships with others. If we want respect, we can practice treating others with respect. If we want to be treated with kindness and compassion, then we can practice extending it to others. If we want environmental sensitivity in the world, we can start by practicing it. If we want financial wealth, we can practice sound measures that are consistent with the core lessons (e.g. we won't steal, embezzle or defraud to improve our own station at someone else's expense). Whatever our goals in life may be, and my message is not intended to discredit or to discount the importance of goals that may differ from my own, I believe that they can be achieved without sacrificing the core lessons that I celebrate here in my writing.

In organizing my thoughts into what might eventually become a book, I found that they were taking form mainly through poetry. I had dabbled in the medium for several years pending my anticipated retirement from the law, and I began to rework some of the poems I had already written and to compose new ones that reflected themes I was beginning to explore. While I preface each poem in this collection with a brief contextual note, or "musing," written at the time of assembling the collection in its present form, my main focus in conveying my reflections has been on the poems, most of which celebrate peaceful co-existence through love, friendship and devotional commitment.

The title of this collection, *Late Winter Sun*, is not only an experience I have tried to capture in my lead-off poem of the same name, it also serves as a metaphor for the light of understanding that dawns in the winter of one's life-cycle. Given the context of this post-retirement project, which I have already introduced in some detail, it seemed to me to be a fitting choice for the collection. I appreciate that not everyone will agree with me about the existence or predominant importance of what I consider to be core lessons for living. But if you are at all intrigued, please read on. If, through the poems and musings I have penned, I am able not only to strengthen my own commitment to the lessons I have chosen to follow, but also to impart a small measure of support to others who may share or become inspired by my faith in them, and who choose to apply them in their own lives, I will consider my retirement journey, my walk in the "late winter sun," to be doubly worthwhile.

LATE WINTER SUN

My wife, Barbara, and I moved to the country in the summer of 2005. It was a pre-retirement decision. I was at the time expecting to retire within three years at most, and the small island community we chose on the Ottawa River in Eastern Ontario promised to be a wonderful spot to retire to. It is a small condominium development in a quasi-resort setting, a place where we had been guests several times in prior years.

Barbara had grown up in a small rural community in New Brunswick before leaving home to attend nursing school in the city at the tender age of 17, whereas I had lived in towns and cities all my life. The water was a big attraction for both of us. Both had lived near water in our youth, and for many years we had owned together a summer cottage on a mid-sized lake in New Brunswick. Living on an island, joined to the mainland only by a short causeway, and having water within a stone's throw on either side of our condo, seemed idyllic. We quickly sold our family home in Ottawa, in which we had resided for the previous 20 years, and moved into our small island condo. Our three children were by then living on their own, so we had already entered a new phase of our married life.

There is a peace and beauty about rural living that I find enchanting. I vividly recall a warm, sunny morning in late March, during the first spring that we lived on the island. Barbara and I seated ourselves on the verandah of the historic log lodge resting on our island property and watched the river begin to break up. Thousands of Canada geese were on the river that morning, some floating on the open water, others parked in groups on the many ice floes that were moving down river. The scene was remarkable. The morning air was filled with boisterous honking sounds as the geese once again played joyfully on their river playground, after a long flight from the south.

Spring river break-up is a time the residents here look forward to each year. Although the setting for *Late Winter Sun* predates the re-opening of the river in the year it was written, it foreshadows the anticipated event. It also recognizes that Barbara and I have entered the "winter" of our own life-cycles, and reflects our appreciation of the blessings we enjoy from these experiences of nature's ebb and flow.

I have chosen this poem to begin the collection because it gives insight into who and where we are today, and sets the scene for themes I will revisit throughout this collection.

Late Winter Sun

The late winter sun breaks through the grey morning skyline,
promising warmth to chase the lingering snow.
Each day runs longer now
and the wind holds less bitterness than before.
The river ice welcomes the sun's rays,
knowing that soon its frozen crystals will dissolve,
freeing them to join the current flowing underneath.
In appreciation, the surface sparkles,
reflecting varied hues of sky above.
Watching quietly, he senses a hint of spring coming.

He knows that soon the geese will return
to preside over the river's breakup.
Honking voices will again fill the night air
as by thousands they shout their triumphant return,
riding ice floes downriver in an avian regatta.
At sunrise they will rise in flight to farmers' fields
to feast on the remnants of last autumn's harvest.
He contemplates the cycle,
predictable, repetitive, year after year,
yet somehow unique in its unfolding each time.

They walk along a country road, the two of them,
enjoying the warmth of the soft southern breeze,
the sun erasing from the pavement traces of white
missed by the hasty scraping of plows days earlier.
She points to a caterpillar crawling across their path,
unsure perhaps of its re-entry into nature's world.
Tiny brooks and streams have come alive,
draining pastures to the river below.

The mood is vibrant, yet peaceful;
the earth is awakening, as is meant to be.

He knows it is winter for them now,
and while seasons repeat in endless rhythm,
in consciousness it is but a moment in time
that we enter and exit the cycle of life.
He knows it is time to enjoy the warmth and comfort,
the reassurance and pleasure of the late winter sun.
And so he savours each step along the roadway with her,
his lifelong love and companion,
confident that whatever late winter storms may still blow past,
this gift of sunshine will carry them to another spring.

THE CHATEAU

When people ask me where I live, I resist saying that I reside outside the village of Lefaivre, which practically no one has heard of. Now I tell them that I live on the Ottawa River, on the Ontario side, directly across from the Chateau Montebello, which is a Quebec landmark that practically everyone in and about Ontario and Quebec is aware of. The Chateau is a magnificent log structure, built around 1930 as the home of the Seigneury Club, an upscale men's retreat for Montreal's business elite (as well as some from Ottawa and elsewhere). The spacious lodge on our own island, often referred to as a Chateau in miniature, was built around the same time, as a summer home by the then owner of the island, lumber baron J.R. Booth, in retaliation, as the legend goes, for his controversial expulsion from the Club for unseemly behaviour. Whether the legend carries any truth is a matter of conjecture, but it certainly speaks of a different age that captures one's imagination, and instills a longing for insight into it.

The Chateau has since become a resort hotel, with its sprawling lawns, luxury features and amenities, attracting guests from around the world. Initially it was a Canadian Pacific Railway hotel, and more recently it has become part of the Fairmont chain of luxury hotels. It continues to be meticulously maintained, and is seen as a playground during all four seasons of the year. It was the site in 2007 of the North American summit of the leaders of Canada, the United

States and Mexico, and the presence of President Bush for a day saw the imposition of an unprecedented security press over the entire region, including our small island. Although we hardly considered our island to be a likely launching pad for a terrorist attack on the Chateau and the leaders camped out there, the security forces were taking no chances. We were placed under a lock-down, and overrun by police, to our bemusement and entertainment.

In truth, the Chateau, with its mystique, is seen by us as part of the charm of our island community. It can easily be accessed by foot or skis over the frozen river in winter, and by boat or auto ferry in summer and fall. It is within full view of the island, and invites vicarious participation in its varied activities. The bright lights, the drifting music, the folks strolling across the grounds, all contribute to scenes that might have sprung from the pages of a novel by F. Scott Fitzgerald.

My poem *The Chateau* was written sometime after Barbara and I had accompanied friends to a banquet held there early in the summer of 2009, and was in part inspired by the pleasant time we had enjoyed on that visit. However, my imagination has wandered well past that singular event to capture romantic notions that one can readily associate with such a setting, and can confidently assume are played out by inspired lovers who seek out the Chateau in order to bask in the magic of its mood.

The Chateau

The Chateau rests at the foot of shallow hills,
its rustic charm complementing the autumn colours.
Smoke trails from the stone flue
as the embers of the evening fire emit their dying gasp
and bid the rising sun to chase the early morning chill.

He sees it clearly, the Chateau,
gazing across the river from his writing desk.
The still water reflects in perfect detail
the inverse of this majestic sight,
too rich to capture in his written word.

He recalls the magic when darkness falls
on warm summer evenings,
lights shimmering across the slowly moving river,
music wafting across open water,
Gatsbyesque memories awakening.

He imagines friends gathering there,
eating, drinking wine, walking in the rain,
sitting around the piano singing songs,
sharing dreams,
tasting pleasures of another age.

He imagines lovers meeting there
in a romantic get-away,
strolling through gardens,
laughing, holding hands, embracing,
lying as one in a dimly lit room.

He imagines being there with her,
sharing heartfelt conversation over tea,
feeling the passion of innocence in her presence
knowing love will never escape
the defended borders of his mind.

The sun in the southern sky beckons to the west wind,
churning quiet waters into spears of white
that dissolve the reflection of a grander life.
He shifts his eyes from the Chateau to his page
and slowly lifts his pen to write.

CASTLES

While the previous comments and poems reflect where I am, now that I have retired, *Castles* is a retrospective on where I have spent most of my professional life. It recalls how easy it is to lose perspective while embedded in the fray of life, and reminds how vital it is to remain grounded.

I grew up with very idealistic notions about the law. However, after being immersed in the legal profession as a lawyer for several years, I became exposed to its many "warts," some of them very troubling to me. I am certain that professionals in other disciplines – medicine, education, science, politics, religion - have parallel reservations about their own "castles" and their roles on the inside of what may appear on their face to be stunning edifices.

For several years of my career I worked as a "law reformer." We were a cadre of idealistic lawyers from across Canada who recognized that much of the law was in need of reform, and who believed that with effort, vision and money, a better "castle" could emerge. Some of our work resulted in modest incremental changes made by legislatures and judges, which may well have proven moderately beneficial. I would not say, however, that overall it has left us with a stronger and more functional "castle" than before. Access to its doors remains financially problematic for most citizens; it takes forever to wind through its corridors; and the end results often bear no relation to the time, cost, effort and stress involved in getting there. Innocent people continue to be convicted of crimes, and while scientific advances such as DNA have helped to free a few of them after long periods of incarceration, the human tragedies are irreversible.

Without doubt, the legal castle can be a brutal place in which to find oneself. Our essential societal response to crime has changed little. While we no longer hold public hangings of persons convicted of minor crimes like stealing a loaf of bread – the last recorded instance in Canada was, I believe, in the 19th century - the system continues to be highly punitive. Yes, the death penalty has been abolished in Canada and across much of the United States, but imprisonment remains a predominant response to convictions. In Western society, Canada is exceeded only by the United States in its use of imprisonment as a penalty. Although the physical conditions of imprisonment have improved over time, a culture of human indignity lingers. Some nations have come to recognize that imprisonment is a costly and dehumanizing way to treat citizens who break the rules, and should be used primarily to restrain individuals who would likely pose a danger to others, should they remain at large. Regrettably, many Canadian politicians today lean towards imposing longer sentences, expanding prison capacity and cutting back on parole eligibility, all under a populist "tough on crime" agenda driven by an apparent thirst for retribution and an illusory quest for deterrence. This prevails in spite of warnings from criminologists that it is a costly, retrograde, and potentially damaging approach.

Compared with advances in science, education, industry, technology, psychology and sociology over the years, it seems that the "rule of law" has evolved relatively slowly in its contribution towards a respectful society. Still, I am comforted that no castle walls are impervious to a deeper truth. This is evidenced by the many positive initiatives and efforts, too numerous to detail in this brief comment, undertaken by remarkable "white knights" within the legal profession who have drawn Light into the "castle" to illumine the way for those needing help. I applaud them!

Castles

The castles of this world,
its structures, systems,
organizations and operations,
all shift and succumb,
decay and eventually dissolve,
to lie undefined in a desert of dust.

None survives the tolling of time,
the complexity of change,
the pursuit of progress.
Briefly populating perceptions of place,
they soon fade into obscurity,
vanishing from view.

Mind conceives of them a short while,
for purposes good and ill,
then dreams of new and better ways
to project grander illusions,
each born to suffer the fate
of its cerebral forebears.

And so castles come and go,
assigned to historical archives
that record their distorted images,
mere shadows of what they were
and the part each played for a period
in the course of consciousness.

Tread carefully through castles, dear friend,
and surrender not your soul to gain entry.
For truth lies beyond their portals,
they being mere passages
through life's labyrinth
on your journey home.

Let integrity temper your inspiration,
and honesty steer your path onward.
Be not tempted to surrender trust
in the pure values that have led you here.
Honour your heart in the choices you make
and be true to your loving self.

CHANGE

I grew up with change. My dad was a railway man, and our family moved frequently from town to town, province to province. I looked forward to it. I was in and out of many schools, but I always seemed to adapt well, even when we moved mid-year – a common enough occurrence for families in those days, but less so today. I attended three universities, and, as a married man, I have lived in 9 homes and have held down 11 different jobs.

Having our three children leave home (over a wide spread of years) and enter the world to fly solo was a huge change for both Barbara and me. We have experienced both heartache and joy over the years, as each of them has had ups and downs on their roads to fulfilled independence. Change is a lifetime process. Parents are parents forever, and seem fated to experience vicariously the range of emotions flowing from changes in their children's lives, as much as their own.

Our friend Paul's passing (memorialized later in this collection) marked a big change for me; and, to a lesser extent, the recent deaths and serious illnesses of other friends, some older, some younger than I, have brought the reality of change into my heightened awareness. Death is the ultimate change for all of us, and yet we understand so little about it and often have such a hard time dealing with it. We fear the change it brings, in spite of the fact that we all know it is coming to us, and to our loved ones, at some point ahead. Perhaps the fear is in not knowing when or how it will occur, what its impact will be, and what lies beyond.

The relocation of friends also brings change that is unavoidable in today's world, even though remaining in touch, electronically and even face-to-face, is so much easier and affordable than it was 20 years ago. Still, the loss of physical proximity can prompt fear that the relationship will change, and may end sometime in the future, leaving the friend lost to us in life, as much as in death.

Retirement has brought about significant changes in my life. Adjusting to the absence of employment's disciplined routine has by-and-large been an easy transition, as my work ethic seems to have shifted my commitment in different directions. Old habits die hard, as they say. Adjusting to a reduced revenue stream dictates a number of life-style changes and eliminates choices that may have been there before. On the other hand, increased flexibility, and having more time to spend with friends and family, are positive aspects of this change - to say nothing of the freedom to accept new opportunities and experiences yet unforeseen.

Overall, change and its implications have been much more in the forefront of my mind in recent years than they were when I was younger and more accepting of the *adventure* and normalcy of change. The adventure part has since been superseded by the drama and emotion of change. Change is definitely more difficult for me to embrace, today. In spite of the unrelenting negative pull of change, which I must reign in from time to time, I try to maintain a positive outlook.

Some may read this poem as an expression of faith in the after-life, upon losing a dear one; others may read it as an expression of optimism for the renewal of an interrupted, yet cherished, friendship. Either way, its message may serve to soften the perceived pain of change.

Change

I feel it sweep over my soul
as I watch the ice surrender to the spring flow.
The continuous reshaping of the river
gently running through my line of sight
reminds me that nothing stays as it was,
the waters and I each destined
for a new tomorrow.

This feeling brings to mind dear ones
since left for distant places.
Receding memories of intimate moments
and fading clarity of those that linger
heighten my sensitivity to winds of change
that whisper: "time is ever spent
and cannot be reclaimed."

Still, there is a calmness about change,
a peace that comes with understanding
that each day offers new perspective,
a restored confidence that when we meet again,
as certain we shall,
there await riches to be mined,
and love and laughter to be shared.

THE RAINS

While vacationing in Northwest Florida in the winter of 2009 I was awakened one night by violent thunderstorms and monsoon-like rains. It was an odd experience for someone from a part of Canada where, in winter, blizzards and freezing temperatures are the norm. Rarely if ever would we see a thunderstorm in January. Even for Florida, the severity of the January storm was somewhat exceptional, with widespread flooding following in its immediate aftermath.

As is usually the case, the storm was followed next day by warm sunny weather that uplifted my spirits, reminding me how closely weather and emotions share their cyclical patterns. Our darkest moments are often forebears of new love, hope and prosperity.

A day later I sat down to try to capture the mood in *The Rains*, taking, of course, a generous slice of "poetic licence" in painting the topographical environs. The exercise brought to mind past stormy interludes in my life, which, in retrospect, had cleared dark air and opened the way for light, for healing and for better times. One of these surrounded a very frightening car accident that Barbara was involved in years ago in New Brunswick. Although it might well have been fatal, and immediately sent fears racing through my mind about how detrimentally life-changing for both of us it could be, she recovered extremely well, and quickly. Her positive attitude throughout the entire hospital experience was an inspiration to me, and ultimately was the catalyst that moved me onto the spiritual path I have continued to follow to this day.

Yes, there were a few rocky moments during the post-hospital recovery period when my coping mechanisms were compromised by fatigue and self-indulgence, but as I looked back on the experience from my contemporary Florida vantage point, I could see in it an affirmation of the truth that hope springs from the worst of situations, if only we can keep our thoughts positive and focused on healing.

The Rains

The rains came hard last night,
washing away the foothold
the sun had gained in the past fortnight.
Water fell in sheets,
illumined by lightning strikes,
encouraged by the endless roar
of thundering applause.

The rains cleansed the sky
and nourished the arid soil.
In the early morning light
buds sprang from branches,
drawing moisture from the air,
turning the world green,
fit once again to sustain life.

Fog now hovers over the moistened earth
as if in sacred blessing,
shrouding the hills in a misty cloak.
The sun fights to restore its foothold,
tempting us to venture forth
to view the transformation
the rains have made.

The rains are as new love,
eclipsing the pain of past hurt,
bringing comfort to anguished souls
who had lost faith.
Pure and regenerating,
each unleashes eternal energy,
renewing the promise of hope.

HOPE

The theme of hope, dominant in *The Rains*, is one I had addressed more directly in the month previous to our trip to Florida in January 2009. I had started by exploring the notion of *expectations*, which is a prominent component of several of today's popular spiritual thought systems. There are many who believe that the manifestation of our dreams is hastened by expectation. If we want a better dream, the first step is to expect that it will manifest. I can see that followers of the very popular teaching "The Secret," and practitioners of "Mastermind," might place a higher value on expectations than on hope.

For me, hope is an inspirational concept, allowing room for acceptance of "what is," and of the miracle that can transform perceptions of "what is" into a different, more loving experience. "I can see this situation differently" is for me a powerful affirmation of the power of the mind to see beyond appearances, and to transcend even the fixed expectations of a better dream. The daunting question for me is this: Can our minds ever see enough of the entire picture to allow us to truly know what dreams we want to manifest? It is one thing to expect, or to hope for, abstract notions such as love, happiness and inner peace. It is another to visualize, or to expect, or to hope for, a concrete scene or situation that will bring about those enhanced states of being. "Be careful what you wish for" is a popular cautionary expression that captures that reservation. Expecting, or hoping for, material enhancement may not bring the love, happiness and peace we *truly* crave.

My reflections in *Hope* are not intended to resolve the mysteries surrounding our experience of the journey of life and the realization of dreams, only to provide food for thought about the situations we seem to inhabit. Although in the poem I place *hope* above *expectations* as a path to peace and contentment, I recognize that words are only symbols, carry differing meanings for different people, and are coloured by individual experiences.

Hope

Expectations beg disappointment.
How peaceful life would be
if we could give them back,
let them go,
or just place them on a shelf
and learn to love,
unconditionally,
accepting all that seems to happen
as mere landmarks
on our journey Home.

Hope inspires,
bringing the miracle of sight
to a sea of illusions.
It is the spark of life,
regenerating when expectations falter.
Only with hope
can we let expectations go,
learn to love unconditionally,
see beyond the landmarks,
discover who and where we are.

THE MESSAGE

Everyone is faced at times with the challenge of offering encouragement. Family or friends fall upon difficult times. Situations that may or may not be of their own making place huge stresses on them. They become discouraged and lose the hope, confidence and sense of self-worth needed to move beyond a crisis. We may feel helpless to respond and, in our desire to comfort, can easily fall into the trap of reinforcing their sense of victimhood. We have all done this, feeling their pain, and wanting to sympathize with them. It is the "rescuer" syndrome. Most psychologists I know or have read would not recommend it as a path to healing.

I wrote *The Message* in such a moment of challenge. It was intended as a message of visioning and hope for someone who, by all objective standards, had been badly treated. To ease my own sense of helplessness, I wrote the poem, hoping that I could bring myself to the point of seeing beyond my own perception of the unfairness of the situation, and that my words might help my friend to change focus.

The Message follows themes expressed elsewhere in this collection, supported as it is by my belief in the power of the mind to think positively and to see differently, even under severe stress.

The Message

"There is Peace in accepting what cannot change,
and Joy in knowing that good times will come.
Though some situations we can't rearrange,
yet in each of them hides an invisible 'plum'."

That is his message to ease her grief,
learning that sadness has gripped her soul.
He hears her heart cry out for relief
as the pain of disappointment takes its toll.

How faint we feel when expectations fail
and dreams dissolve like morning mist.
How futile seems the hardened trail
toward the illusionary abyss.

He knows it is time to lift his hand
to shift the gaze of her burdened eyes.
And so he writes, praying she will understand
that always with Faith will come a prize.

It behoves dear friends to point the way
to loved ones blind to the future they own.
However far her hope should stray,
may his message be heard to guide it home.

REALITY

My previous musings on change, hope, expectations and positive
thinking lead inevitably into a discussion of "reality." What is real
and what is illusion? I have come to understand that what we call
"reality" is actually *experience*, rather than *fact*. Yes, our experience
confirms that there are "facts" that appear to be fixed and beyond
change. However, do those facts dictate what is real? I believe
that we can change our reality through our thoughts, by choos-
ing to experience our world, and the facts and situations that we
face, differently.

We grew up being taught in school about "scientific" fact, but
looking back on how much has changed of that so-called "reality"
over my lifetime I feel quite comfortable in my frequent assertion
that science is just another way of seeing the world. We are taught to
experience the world within a defined, but ever-changing, scientific
framework. However, that does not make for an immutable reality.

In the same vein, I view my own profession, law, as just another
way of seeing the world. It affords a framework, or rather many
frameworks, within which we can view and assess relationships
amongst the many varied interests that can be identified as claim-
ing attention within our global and domestic societies. But in the
end, law is no more or less "real" than science. Much the same
can be said about religion, which, at different points in our evolu-
tion, and even now in some parts of the world, has been closely

associated with both law and science. The same holds for medicine, the "reality" of disease and its relief being viewed very differently across ages and cultures.

All of these frameworks of experience, which are commonly thought of as "reality," are the product of human thought, which invariably changes. At the global or societal level, it can be a slow and difficult process to shift thought into a new experience of reality. That said, paradigm-changing events - the discovery of fire, the invention of the wheel, the agricultural revolution, the development of writing, the invention of the printing press, the industrial revolution, the educational revolution, the harnessing of nuclear energy, the information age, the technological revolution - have each accelerated changing perceptions of reality, at an ever-increasing pace. In the result, today's "reality" will soon be yesterday's historical anachronism; it was ever thus and ever shall be.

At the individual level, a reality shift is relatively more manageable, as long as one has confidence in the power of thought and the discipline to control one's mind. Each of us can choose to see differently. This is the realm of miracles, which are accessible to all, not just the saints. The key to re-visioning, I believe, is to find the universal thread that connects us all, which is the only true reality. It has been described in many ways throughout history. In my poem *Reality*, I have called it Love. Others may recognize it by a different name.

Reality

There is no world
but the world I see,
and what I see
is "reality."

There is no "you"
but the "you" I see,
and the "you" I see
is who you'll be.

There is no "me"
but the "me" you see,
and the "me" you see
is who I'll be.

For the world you see
is your reality,
unfolding before you,
exclusively.

In different strokes
we paint each day
with inner shades
that colour our way.

Neither can see
through the other's eyes,
or feel the pain
'neath their lonely cries.

Can we not transcend
our reality?
How do we bond
in solidarity?

Love is the way
we become aware,
disrobing illusion
with truth we can share.

AGED LOVE

L*ove* is a word that is used in so many contexts, with such widely differing intentions, that it would be futile to try to give meaning to it in any universal sense. In prehistoric times, when survival trumped romance, it likely was an unknown concept. But with the growth of civilization volumes have been written on the topic, and it has been thoroughly explored in the major media over the centuries. I use the word in various ways, depending on the circumstances, both in conversation and in my writing. In my poem *The Rains*, for example, I used it more in the traditional sense of romantic love. In *Reality* and several other poems I used it with a more Divine connotation. At best I can only offer a glimpse into what love actually means to me in its purest sense, within the deepest part of me. That meaning has shifted considerably over the course of a lifetime: - what I once thought to be love, and felt to be love, I no longer identify with love, or at least with what I sometimes refer to in my writing as "true" love, or "Love."

The complexity of meaning surrounding the word is exacerbated by the presence of sex, often referred to as *making* love. While love and sexual attraction can coexist, they are quite independent feelings, and can and do stand alone. As we can all observe in what we read and view in the media, and in ordinary life, having sex is not necessarily about love. It can become just a recreational activity, a way of massaging ego, a control/power exercise, a war crime, or all of these and more. I am confident that readers are well aware of the destructive roles sex has played over the ages: - it may well vie with religion and recreational drugs for recognition as the most destructive influence in the history of civilization. While its constructive roles can hardly be overlooked, it is equally apparent how easily sex can *get in the way of* experiencing love in its purest form. Perhaps it is only when sex is *not* an element of a relationship that we can accurately gauge the nature and depth of our love for another.

In *Aged Love* I have tried to capture love that has transcended sexual tensions and entered a peaceful domain, a deeper and truer love than was ever imagined in my youth.

Aged Love

There is comfort in aged love,
well cured over a lifetime together.
Beyond the challenges of parenthood
and the strains of self-indulgence,
love opens onto a peaceful landscape
where small blessings are understood,
received and appreciated.

I note them often, in quiet moments,
a stroll aside the river's edge,
a drive along pretty country roads,
lunch at a quaint village inn.
I feel the contentment of togetherness,
the healing balm of acceptance,
the inner joy of being.

It has soul, this aged love,
like the rich tones of a vintage guitar,
mellow and mature to my ear,
its seasoned wood
none the worse for weathered cracks,
vibrating softly in my hands,
massaging memories with its resonance.

Aged love sheds the complexity of young love,
the uncertainty of meaning,
the minefield of painful regrets,
the struggle for respect and honesty.
Who has stayed the long course
from blind promise of love
finds now what was then unimagined.

THE WORDS/ THE
UNSPOKEN TRUTH

To continue the discussion of love, the words "I love you" are often spoken so feely in today's society that they seem meaningless. How often do we encounter them in casual conversation on TV, in movies and in ordinary day to day life? They may be spoken in friendly affection, or in expressing simple gratitude, or, on the dark side, disingenuously, in an attempt to manipulate a relationship. The context in which the words are spoken is key to interpreting the meaning they are intended to carry. They often have nothing to do with "love," in its more usual connotations.

The other side of the coin is that some people have difficulty speaking the words in a serious relationship, perhaps for fear of commitment or simply because they grew up in an environment where loving emotions and words of endearment were rarely present. Many dramatic stories have been written about women who long to hear those words from the man they love, highlighting the frustration, doubt, pain, disappointment and sometimes tragedy that can flow from the refusal to speak them. Relationships have died because fear has silenced these words.

In the two, somewhat related, poems that follow, I have tried to capture the importance of seeing beyond verbal communication to experience underlying love in other ways. When love is there, even though muted, it is possible to see and feel what remains unspoken, and to find peace in the silence. Love, in its purest form, is dependent neither on sexual expression, nor on the spoken word. It simply and naturally exudes, enriches, comforts and heals.

The Words

The words come easily to her,
the natural expression of feelings
that run deep and true,
flowing from the soul connection
she has felt from the onset of their time together.

The words come effortlessly.
"I love you" seems so pure and honest.
How could fear silence the truth of feelings
that her heart confirms
to be the essence of her being?

For him, the words are less comfortable.
For reasons that are part of his life's journey,
he cannot speak them,
fearing that to do so may lessen his claim
on the freedom he so values.

She understands, and does not recant.
For although the words are unspoken,
when she looks into his eyes and welcomes his touch,
she feels the love that underlies,
and knows it is there, always.

The Unspoken Truth

Their lips have not touched,
and his are sealed to the unspoken truth.
Yet, she looks through his eyes into his heart
and sees the intensity,
purity and innocence
of the love that is held inside.

And so is revealed the unspoken truth,
received in silent gratitude,
acknowledging a divine connection that God has blessed,
and released from the bonds of time and space.

DISTANCE

For several years while I was attending university a half century ago, Barbara and I had what is today referred to as a "long distance" relationship. She was in nursing school, over a hundred miles away. Traveling those miles by bus or thumb was not easy for me. Consequently, weeks often passed between times we could be together. This was long before the days of cell phones and email, so communication was almost exclusively by post. I would write to her and she would write back, and then I'd reply. And so the cycle went. I recall descending the stairs to the residence mail room on days when I calculated that a response was due. Sometimes I was rewarded with a letter; sometimes I came away disappointed. How crushed, sad and doubting I felt when a reply was overdue by a few days and I returned empty-handed! However, always there was eventual communication, and so we managed to survive that period of our relationship. Barbara still has stored away, somewhere, a pile of letters I wrote to her over that period of our lives.

Long distance relationships are common today, not just with students studying away from home, but with professionals whose careers can land them at different ends of the country, or of the globe. The difference today is that internet communication is instantaneous, and air travel is frequent, quick and relatively affordable. How different and difficult it was for soldiers and their wives and families in times past. Months, sometimes years, passed without any communication. Barbara's uncle, for instance, was imprisoned and isolated in a Japanese prisoner of war camp during most of World War II. Still, his bride-to-be stood by him in faith that he would return. They eventually married after the war and lived together into their old age. I am sure that stories like that one abound amongst our veterans.

There is undoubtedly a difference of opinion as to whether the ability to communicate instantaneously makes long-distance relationships easier today than they were in former years. Some may argue that it doesn't make them any easier. Doubts and insecurities can surface when texts, emails or voicemail messages are not returned promptly. The tone of a quick message may foster misinterpretation. The quickness of the chosen medium may sometimes deter thoughtful and sensitive communication. Human insecurities seem neither to be solved nor salved through technology.

I wrote *Distance* with those in mind who struggle with long distance relationships. In line with my explorations of reality, illusion and the power of thought, it occurred to me that I had a perspective to share that might relieve some of their anxiety. If time and space are only illusions, as I believe they are, it follows that distance must be part of the illusion. If one chooses to see through the eyes of Love, anything can be seen differently, even being physically apart.

Distance

Distance is the space between two hearts,
as near or far as either chooses,
unrelated to the linear measure
of earthly experience.

Distance is the incongruity of minds
that conceive they are apart,
oblivious to the connections
through which thought is shared.

Distance is the disharmony of souls
whenever Truth is absent,
moving ever apart on dissonant scales,
the melody yet unheard.

Distance is illusion
to hearts that beat together,
to minds that find connection,
to souls that know True Love.

MAKING TURKEY SOUP

Although I have been blessed with good health throughout my life, there were occasional times when I would fall ill. Whenever this happened, I was always pampered, first by my mother and later by Barbara. However, my bouts of ill health were so infrequent that I never really developed a sensitivity to illness in others, or empathy for what they were going through. It has long been a bone of contention between Barbara and me that I can never seem to relate to her needs when she falls ill. Perhaps it is because I have never experienced the degree of incapacity that she suffers whenever she succumbs to a bug. In my defence, I can only say that when Barbara gets sick, she really gets sick, to the point that I feel totally helpless to do anything that could possibly make her feel better. I have sung to her from time to time, and have occasionally rubbed her feet, but ministering to the sick has never been my strong suit. Mother Teresa I am not!

So it definitely seemed uncharacteristic of me, when Barbara came down with a post-Christmas flu recently, to think about making turkey soup for her. Perhaps it was because I had remembered her preparing soup in the past to nurse our children back to health. Whatever the motivation, I had a strong urge to do this for her. It seemed to be a loving gesture I could offer.

I gathered together the vegetables and other ingredients, stripped some left-over meat off the turkey, and sat down for the next two hours putting it all together in a pot to simmer on the stove. For me it was a transformative moment, a wonderful new experience. However, as good as the soup turned out to be, I soon discovered that it was not something Barbara was in any condition to enjoy. I confess that this was a bit of a downer for me. I had thought that sipping turkey soup was a sure remedy for ill health; unfortunately, it turns out I was mistaken.

Yes, there was momentary disappointment on my part that Barbara had not been as appreciative as I had expected she might be. The feeling passed, however, as I remembered the love I had felt in making the soup, and as I reminded myself that if love is given unconditionally, it is not dependant on having someone else accept it.

I was motivated to pen *Making Turkey Soup* because it had been such a moving moment for me, and because I believed that, in spite of appearances, there was a measure of healing in the experience, for both of us. Even though I recognized that Barbara's consciousness, in that moment, was not entirely in the space reflected in the closing stanza of the poem (which would have optimized my story), I did sense a faint expression of gratitude from her that I had at least made the effort to please her. I think that if you were to ask her today, she would readily acknowledge the love that I had poured into her bowl that evening.

Making Turkey Soup

Few things in life are as satisfying
as making turkey soup
for a loved one
who is ill.
It's a meditation of thanks
for healing,
for sustenance,
for the grace of giving.

Sliced carrots,
diced onions
a cup of rice,
chopped celery and spice.
Each adds its unique flavour
to the remnants of meat
picked from the boiled bones
of the one who surrendered.

Even though your loved one
may have no appetite,
she will sip her bowl in quiet appreciation
of the gesture you have made.
For she knows that healing is not in the mix,
nutritious and delicious as it seems to you,
but in the love that inspired
the making of turkey soup.

MOMENT OF TRUTH

I write consistently about love, because I believe it is such a hopeful and healing state of being and becoming. And yet, it can equally be a source of pain and disillusionment. Books, movies and songs are filled with stories of love lost, love gone wrong, love unrealized, unrequited love, and on and on. People relate to the pain of love, perhaps because we have all experienced it and can take comfort in the fact that the experience is universal. In today's world we see high divorce rates, unimaginable domestic violence, and rampant infidelity, all of which appear to negate the healing power of love.

It is no secret that love is not necessarily a bed of roses. In loving relationships there is a key junction (or several) that I have called a "moment of truth." It may be a moment that few besides the partners themselves know about. To many, if not most, observers, Barbara and I probably appear to be a model married couple. Yet we both know that we have had our "moments of truth." Few couples have not. Some have come through it; many have not.

Love cannot mature, flourish and achieve a pure state of "true" love without forgiveness. Forgiveness can be a hard thing to extend, because most of us have been taught over a lifetime that it is an indulgence to be given to the other person, rather than a gift to ourselves. We resist forgiving, because we think the other person has hurt us and does not deserve our forgiveness. But if we can see differently, if we can forgive the other person in order to heal ourselves, resistance fades. The act of forgiving heals. Try it! The other person will heal with you; both of you will let go of the moment of truth, and love will be freed to re-enter the relationship. Today, more and more is being written on the healing power of forgiveness, much of it emphasizing the point of view I have just expressed and is reflected in the poem that follows.

Moment of Truth

It comes in every loving relationship,
a moment of truth
when illusions dissolve,
when the closeness that seemed to be
evaporates
as the fear of honesty takes hold.

The moment may follow angry words,
a sense of betrayal
or benign inattentiveness.
One heart turns on the other,
and what seemed to be unified, divides,
each part seeking shelter in its own space.

Reconciliation may restore illusion,
and a smile rekindle kind words.
But neither overcomes the thought,
terrifying in that moment,
that every heart beats separately,
and every soul rests alone with God.

Yet, there is a healing moment
that only Faith knows,
a moment of pure forgiveness.
As one heart opens honestly to the other
the two will beat again as one,
and Truth will usher Love's return.

TRUE FRIENDSHIP

Loving relationships are not confined to conjugal ones; they can encompass relationships with offspring, siblings and other relatives. Expanding the circle even further is the love that can exist between friends.

"Friendship," like "love," is a word that is used in so many different ways and contexts it is impossible to ascribe any single meaning to it. As a young lawyer, an expression that amused me was "my learned friend." Lawyers frequently use it in court settings, often while putting down opposing lawyers with an incisive reference to a case, doctrine or argument trumping their adversaries' prior submissions to the court. I believe that the word "friend" was originally used in this context to affirm a sense of collegiality, recognizing that the ethics of the profession bind lawyers together in a common goal, the pursuit of justice. Too often, I have observed over the years, the expression is used in a condescending, rather than an affirming, way.

In today's world, people are often besieged with requests to become someone's "friend" on Facebook, and on other social networking websites. How often does a request come from someone you don't include within your circle of friends, or whose name you don't even recognize? On the one hand, the practice can perhaps be seen as supporting the ideal that people should be willing to befriend everyone they meet in the world, a noble thought for sure but probably beyond most people's common understanding of the word. On the dark side, acquiring social networking "friends" can become an ego-enhancing exercise, with "friends" being routinely collected in a competitive way: - "I have five-hundred 'friends' on my page. How many do you have?" I often wonder how disappointing it is for someone, having requested another as a friend, not to get a response.

I wish also to acknowledge the "friends of my youth," to recall Robert Penn Warren's phrase in his acclaimed novel *All the King's Men*. These are friends with whom one may share very little in common in later years, except the memory of the close bond formed while growing up together. However, the memory is indelible and can support an enduring, and sometimes irrational, sense of loyalty.

True Friendship honours a bond that I regard as being different again. I see true friendship as a deep and demanding relationship that is felt at the soul level. It is a connection that may come several times in a lifetime, or only once, or never. It must be nurtured. As is the case with most enduring personal relationships, forgiveness is the glue that holds it together. As one who has been blessed with true friendship, I have attempted, in my poem, to capture in words what I believe to be its essential pillars.

True Friendship

It's an attraction of souls,
an opening of hearts,
a meeting of minds,
a commitment of selves.

It rests on five pillars,
sculpted in concert,
maintained daily,
restored with forgiveness.

The first is Honesty,
integrity of word,
reflected in action,
sensitively shared.

The second is Trust,
in both its dimensions,
given in thought
and earned in deed.

The third is Respect,
accepting each other,
knowing perfection
rests only in God.

The fourth is Kindness,
care and support,
heart-felt compassion
in all said and done.

The fifth is Love,
pure in thought and intent,
innocent in expression,
unconditionally given.

True Friendship is timeless,
has no spatial constraints,
endures all it faces
while its pillars stand firm.

GROWING OLD

If readers will indulge me with a bit of background to my musings on aging, may I humbly suggest that the most fundamental challenge to understanding the meaning of life is the mystery that surrounds *consciousness*. Does consciousness arise from a physical reality, specifically the brain? Does the brain generate a cognitive mind, as Nobel laureate Dr. Eric Kandel believes he has proven in his biological research explaining mind and defining consciousness? Or, as others understand, is what we think of as physical reality (which includes the brain) merely a product of universal mind? This is a debate that arguably is beyond the realm of science, because science is premised on the concrete reality of our physical surroundings. For those who believe that so-called physical reality is but a product of consciousness, a "scientific" answer holds little authority. It comes down to belief. Is the apparent physical world "real," or is what we commonly think of as reality only an ontological "dream," generated by a universal consciousness that embraces mind?

I do not claim to have the answer, although, to confirm suspicions about my own bias, I confess that I lean towards the second explanation. Doubtless we have a compelling experience of reality within the "dream," but it is easy to confuse experience with what is real. In our sleeping dream, for example, we often mistake, at least while in that state, the events of our dream as being real. I do not pretend to comprehend or explain the conundrum, and I accept that it lies beyond the realm of absolute understanding and must rest as an article of faith. A helpful discussion of the issue, which I read some time ago, is a small book written by physicist Peter Russell, entitled *From Science to God*. Do not expect to find definitive answers there, but the discussion is fascinating. The most persuasive spiritual discussion that I have read is in *A Course in Miracles*, which teaches forgiveness and inspires kindness as tools for correcting our misperceptions about who and what we are.

Growing old is something we all face, barring premature death. Death of our bodies is entrenched in our "dream" of reality as a passage in the journey of life that each of us must find a way to deal with. No one escapes it. Growing old has spawned a number of popular expressions such as: "you are only as old as you think." Positive thinking is doubtless an asset in coping with old age. I am doing my best to approach it positively, believing that the demise of my physical body is simply a gateway to a new experience within a deeper consciousness, the nature of which I cannot even imagine today.

Affirming consciousness as "what is real" opens the door to a realm of possibilities, whether reincarnation or, more likely, a state of being of which we can have no comprehension within our current realm of experience. However, I believe that whatever burdens we carry in our minds, and cannot resolve during our life-times, are carried into our next dimension of consciousness. This is why suicide is not a release from emotional pain. This is why, at a personal level, I consider it so important to find ways to bring what I have called the "core lessons" to the forefront of my mind before departing this life. In my poem *Growing Old*, I commend the chal-lenging path of love as the course to follow in order to extend and enrich my days here and to prepare myself for the next experience. All of which is terribly abstract, but such is the nature of Faith, Truth, the meaning of life and, of course, growing old.

Growing Old

There are days I feel I'm growing old,
or perhaps it's just a belief I hold.
Could old age only be illusion,
springing from mere thought confusion?

It is said that brains will slowly age,
causing minds to disengage.
But suppose opposing proof be found,
that minds decide when brains run down?

When minds leave bodies, dead or alive,
do they look for love on the other side?
Do some lose sight of what is here
and shift their gaze to another tier?

Could the secret to not growing old
be keeping thoughts from becoming cold,
allowing love to slow the years,
tempting minds to stay us here?

This is not about sex, no, let me be clear,
rather, having someone we can call dear.
Someone to cherish and welcome with pride,
a sensitive love in whom to confide.

Love's all around, if we open our eyes,
though it's often masked in fear's disguise.
Being able to say and mean "I love you"
can lift the shroud that obscures love's view.

Yet we falter in silence, afraid to commit,
fearing that others will not permit
their hearts to open to invite us in,
leaving us shivering in our naked skin.

The more years advance, the higher the price,
and the harder it seems to heed this advice.
But if there's a will to keep aging at bay
I see no better course than choosing love's way.

DEATH'S PATIENCE

Undoubtedly this will seem a strange title to some, as death, in many tragic cases, seems to be anything but patient. However, in the larger picture, it seems to me that death *is* patient, though inevitably bringing our experience here to a close. I see the process of death as being driven largely by choices, ones we make ourselves and ones that others make that affect us, some of them intentional and some unintentional. Probably most of them are unconscious choices, in the sense that we do not readily associate them with imminent death.

It is sometimes said that we choose to be born and, in so doing, choose our own death. Whether or not there is any truth to the idea that we choose our birth, death can be traced forensically to choices we have made in life, choices about where we are in the moment, what we eat, who we associate with and the risks we run. This does not mean that we necessarily choose the time and means of death. However, in some cases (relatively few but in increasing numbers), people *do* consciously choose when and how they die, for example in suicides, terrorist self-destruction, hunger strikes, and terminal health decisions. On the brighter side, most of us are likely aware of situations in which terminally ill persons have literally willed themselves to live, either by complete self-healing, or by delaying death far beyond the time when physicians have pronounced their imminent demise. That too is a choice.

It is this deference to choice that gives meaning to my notion of death's "patience." And whether the choice is intentional, or random and unpredictable, there is always a choice between life and death that is active at some level of our consciousness, whether we are cognitively aware of it or not. This observation lines up with the idea I had expressed in my comment to my previous poem, *Growing Old,* that death may be part of the mind's "dream" or experience of reality, rather than a dark blank at the end of life's road, as some believe it to be. If so, then it follows that we are the dreamer of our "dream" of life and death, and we exercise choices within the dream.

We live in an age that has seen exponential growth in medical technology, with new and amazing equipment, medication and procedures that are designed to diagnose and treat disease. While not cheating death, in any strict sense, this innovation certainly tests death's patience by delaying its occurrence. The bright side is that technology affords, for many people, new opportunity to enjoy a full and wholesome life, free of disease that previously would have taken years off their lifespan and forced them to live out what remaining years they had in discomfort and disability. The dark side, perhaps, is the capability of technology to prolong life beyond natural expectations, without enhancing measurably the quality of the life that is preserved. Between those opposite ends of the spectrum lie difficult ethical choices for medical professionals, families, caregivers, and patients themselves. Yes, death can be patient, as people struggle with these choices; but at what price, financially, emotionally, physically and spiritually, is our ultimate fate postponed?

My poem *Death's Patience* touches lightly on some of those thoughts.

Death's Patience

Death patiently awaits us all,
for its sentence will outlast
even those who, bent on life,
wriggle in death's grasp.

Although our world spends priceless wealth
to slow this sure release,
eventually it comes to naught,
for the breath of all will cease.

Yet death may grant indulgences,
and delay its angels' calls
on those who choose to stay the course,
postponing what befalls.

Still, those who have forgotten joy
can beg of death, "make haste,
lift me past the horrid stench
of flesh that's gone to waste."

But mostly death does not discern,
or discriminate at all;
random choices seem the measure
of our tenure at the ball.

What lies beyond I cannot say,
death doth no promise make;
a mind that can conceive of death
may yet hover at the wake.

PAUL

Paul was a good friend and neighbour, a beautiful man growing old contentedly, having just celebrated his 70th birthday with his family while vacationing in Mexico. He passed away quite suddenly, after a short illness, in March 2011. I wrote this commemorative poem a few days afterwards, while still in shock over his rapid demise. Paul was someone I had looked forward to spending time with in my retirement. In many ways he embodied the spirit of our small island community, always eager to press forward with new projects, and offering large blocks of his private time to seeing them through.

Paul was one of very few persons with whom I had shared any of my poems. A man of letters, a former English professor, and an avid reader, he had seemed a safe choice to expose myself to. Never one to flaunt his past academic standing and achievements, I knew he would not be judgmental, and might even lend me some confidence to pursue my writing.

Paul's death was a grim reminder of how fragile life can be. A large, strong and active man, he was felled by disease in a relative instant. His passing, which he himself accepted with model grace, provides us with inspiration to make every day count, and to make every communication with others around us as kind and respectful as we would want our final words to be.

Paul (1941-2011)

Death has deprived us of the promise of tomorrow,
good conversation over vintage wine,
friendly walks along nearby trails,
getting to know each other better.

Death has denied us opportunity
to share views on books just read,
to trade ideas about the world
and our beloved space within.

Death leaves me to search in memory
for new insight from past recollections,
affording substance to the ghost left behind,
to visions still vivid in my mind's eye.

Death is a cruel master, yet overcome
by gratitude for past kindnesses,
by acceptance of what is now at rest,
and by loving thoughts of the enduring spirit.

PURE PRESENCE

By now readers will be aware that although I was raised as a boy in the Anglican Church I am not a religious person; nor do I have a mainstream understanding of God. I was jolted when reminded in a recent newspaper article that many fundamentalist Christians believe that one cannot get a passport to heaven unless it has been issued by Jesus (and then only to those who believe in Him), leaving the rest, including some pretty notable humanitarians and spiritual leaders, perpetually consigned to hell. Other religious orders appear to hold similar insular and discriminatory beliefs. That should not be disturbing to those of us who believe that so-called "heaven" and "hell" are states of being, spaces within consciousness that we experience in the *now*, not places awaiting us at the end of our lives on judgment day. But it is of concern, nonetheless.

It is ironic that so many people have died over the centuries, and continue to die, at the hands of religious zealots of many followings and denominations, eager to assert their own idea of a deity above all others. Nothing, not patriotism, tribalism or family loyalty, rivals religious affinity as an incentive to violence, whenever religious beliefs are perceived to be threatened. It seems to make no difference that a religious order may pay lip service to the sanctity of life, and may view killing as sin; the rule may not apply if the victim is seen as an infidel, a non-believer.

Fortunately, in the Western world, we do not live with the extent of physical violence experienced in some parts of the world, but at the level of thought and intent, far too much religious intolerance persists. This is in spite of human rights laws and educational initiatives aimed at stamping out religious discrimination and hate-mongering.

It seems as though there is a latent fear in humans that if they do not defend their respective deities, or if they allow their fundamental religious beliefs to be challenged, their personal security is at risk of evaporating into the ether, leaving them naked and vulnerable to the perils of the universe and the beyond. Perhaps there are more learned psychological explanations of the phenomenon, but it appears to me that zealous belief in an *external* deity has raised daunting challenges for civilizations over the centuries.

I recognize that the zealots to whom I have just referred are extremists, and that millions of people practice mainstream religion of all kinds benignly. It is not my purpose to insult or criticize them, or to deny the ultimate teachings of their religions, which espouse peace, love, respect and harmony as much as I do in my own beliefs and writings. I have simply chosen otherwise, to find God in consciousness, not outside me, by listening for the silent voice of right-mindedness within. My poem *Pure Presence* paints a simple picture of this quiet spiritual practice in search of "heaven" in the here and now.

Pure Presence

Listen quietly,
listen openly,
the voice draws near,
Pure Presence is here.
Don't look outside,
for it "speaks" from inside,
from the core of consciousness
whence God comes to bless.

It's a message of love,
one that carries above
the pursuit of wealth
and promotion of self.
It's a message of giving,
of joyful living;
a call for sharing,
compassion and caring.

Some choose to name it
and exclusively claim it,
but its reign is universal,
the heritage of all.
Some will ignore it,
and even abhor it;
yet those come aware
who surrender to prayer.

Not prayer of asking,
but rather of listening,
free from intrusion
of ego illusion.
While this world struggles on
with hope nigh foregone,
God doth appear,
Pure Presence is here.

CONSCIENCE

"Conscience" is a word I grew up with – "Follow your conscience;" "Do you have a clear conscience?" "He must have a guilty conscience." – yet it was not a concept I had given much thought to. I had always accepted it as being there, a sense of "right" versus "wrong," but I had never stopped to consider where it comes from. It just seemed to be an innate characteristic of the human personality that we have an inner knowing of what is right and what is wrong. Wearing my lawyer hat for the moment, I became acquainted early on with the McNaughton rules for criminal insanity, a branch of which states that no one can be held criminally responsible who, on account of mental illness, is incapable of distinguishing right from wrong. Yet even that awareness did not kindle my interest in digging deeper. In simplified language, the test excludes from criminal conviction those who do not have a conscience. But what is conscience and where does it come from?

As the story of civilization has witnessed, it seems there is only relative truth around "right" and "wrong," as seen through secular eyes. So is conscience merely a reflection of our education, laws, customs and experiences, or does it reflect a deeper moral sense? I note that our law extends reasonable constitutional protection for thought and belief; and our political institutions make room for conscientious objection to certain laws and customs. So there seems to be, at least within our social consciousness, recognition of a non-contextual, spiritual, sense of right and wrong. Recent psychological research suggests that even 8 month old babies will express a sense of justice, suggesting that there may well be an innate source of conscience.

It is puzzling to me that while the vast majority of Western religious doctrines emphasize prayer to an external deity for guidance, practically all of us already possess this inner sense, though often repressed, of what is right and what isn't. I appreciate that religious leaders, and perhaps psychiatrists too, may have ways of explaining it, but I prefer to see it as an element of universal consciousness that our individual minds form a part of. To my simple understanding, there is a "higher" consciousness and a "lower" consciousness: – a sense of "Right-mindedness" and one of "wrong-mindedness" – and we get to choose which we will follow in any given situation. Deep down, if we listen, we know the right choice; yet often we ignore it because of anger, fear, convenience, rationalization, perceived gain, pressure from others, or any number of other reasons that divert us from making the choice for what is right. Regrettably, an errant choice usually leads to a loss of respect for self and others, even when it may not immediately be apparent to us. How easily what I have earlier referred to as the "core lessons" can elude our attention!

Whatever its source may be – and it will ever remain an article of faith, not scientific or spiritual certainty – conscience is something most of us can place within an empirical framework. Like a river, it may be hard to define, but we know one when we see one – as the saying goes. Most of us can feel conscience and recognize its authoritative status, whether we follow it or not.

My poem is a personal commitment to listen more attentively to, and follow the voice of, conscience, as well as an invitation to readers to check in more regularly with their inner voice when faced with challenging choices.

Conscience

Were I the grandest wizard in this land,
with power to change how people understand,
I'd implant this helpful step for them to follow,
else risk the pain that slowly starts to grow:
"Whenever you're unsure what to decide,
always let your conscience be your guide."

This lesson is as old as day's first dawn,
taught to youth by elders early on.
Yet oft forgot as challenges are met,
eclipsed by fears that right will bring regret.
And so, ensuing chaos doth endure
to silence guidance that would speak more pure.

As I approach in age three score and ten,
were I to live those many years again
I'd heed the wisdom only now I see
was far too often laid aside by me.
In conscience would I soothe my troubled soul
and find the path toward a worthy goal.

I've not found God in churches, old or new,
or in sacred temples with a wise guru,
or high above me, looking down to choose
the one who wins, and the one who thus must lose.
No, it's that sense of Right that is only felt within,
that stirs my mind to elude the grip of sin.

From Conscience comes a yearning to respect
myself and those with whom I shall connect
in living out my days, an active soul,
in a wounded world that craves a wizard's role.
As I set sail on the early evening tide,
may I always choose my conscience as my guide.

RESPECT

In my Introduction, and in various comments in this collection, I have repeatedly referred to *respect*. I have put it forward as a key element of what I have identified as core lessons we are to learn. It is doubtless an appropriate time for me to write about respect, in the wake of a vitriolic election campaign in Canada, marked by attack ads, brutal insults and other flagrant evidence of disrespect that have characterized the Canadian political landscape for several years, especially those leading up to the 2011 election. The tone of disrespect in Parliament, and on the hustings, has not escaped the notice of pundits and politicians, and I am encouraged that several elected politicians have recently dedicated themselves publicly to fostering more respectful communication within our Parliamentary system in days ahead. The outpouring of public support, especially from youth, for the late Jack Layton, who was the NDP Official Opposition leader in Parliament for a brief three months following the election, bodes well for a new politics of hope, optimism and, yes, respect.

What also caught my attention recently was a moving CBC interview of Canadian journalist Mellissa Fung, following the debut of her book *Under an Afghan Sky*. In the book she recounts her ordeal of being kidnapped for ransom in Afghanistan in 2008, and her release, having endured 28 days confined in a hole in the ground (literally). In the course of it she experienced some degrading treatment from at least one of her captors. What was so powerful about her interview was her telling how she had since forgiven her captors, and the reason she gave for her extending forgiveness. In spite of the disrespect that had been shown her, she chose not to carry hatred forward as she resumed her life. She chose to heal, and she saw forgiveness as the quickest path to healing. This brought to my mind, and reinforced, comments on forgiveness that I have shared earlier.

The media fanfare over the recent Osama bin Laden killing brings to the fore perhaps the biggest challenge we can have to choosing respect and forgiveness as central elements of a life-path. How can one possibly respect and forgive someone like bin Laden, a self-confessed architect of so much terrorist killing and destruction? Admittedly it is difficult to do. And so I can understand the jubilation and celebration exhibited by many of the kin and friends of those who had lost their lives in the terrorist attacks on the Twin Towers in New York on September 11, 2001. I withhold judgment, and I respect them, not knowing how I might react should I ever be forced to endure what they have endured.

I acknowledge that there are differing schools of thought surrounding the path to healing: some professionals profess that vengeance can be a healthy expression of emotion. Others prefer the path of forgiveness. As readers will appreciate, my choice is for forgiveness, however challenging the situation may be. I believe that somewhere deep down inside all of us, there resides a "child of God," as it is sometimes expressed. It is that element that I believe is deserving of respect. Our disrespect, judgment and unforgiveness towards others only suppress the emergence of this element; whereas our respect nurtures it. Fortunately, in our day-to-day lives, at least in this country, we are not confronted by bin Ladens, and so the practice of respect can often be carried out without the severe challenges of extreme circumstances. If we start small, we can condition ourselves to handle bigger challenges when they occur, as eventually they may.

Respect

Although we come from different worlds,
with different hopes and dreams in view;
I ask you not to stand apart,
for I realize you have a heart
that surely beats like mine.

The different colours of our skin
bespeak the homelands whence we've come;
yet it matters not our hues aren't wed,
for beneath the shells our blood runs red
as if from common source.

We may speak in different tongues,
with words not fully understood;
yet there's no cause to silence speech,
for it carries culture shared by each
with those who choose to hear.

We may hold long-taught beliefs
of separate paths to godliness;
yet the voice of Conscience overlays,
and though expressed in different ways,
each message is in tune.

There may be times I won't approve
and can't condone what you have done;
yet will I treat you with respect,
for the better judge of what's correct
is the quiet Voice within.

You may not always be inclined
to reciprocate respect for me;
yet will I not then treat you worse,
for I choose to hinder hatred's curse
from weighing on my mind.

KINDNESS

I have identified respect and kindness as key elements of the core lessons. I celebrated respect in my previous poem. *Kindness* takes the teaching to a higher level. It is one thing to treat others with respect; it is yet another to be kind to them. Respect is predominantly a state of mind, an attitude that inspires politeness. Kindness requires a higher level of affirmative action. I have met several kind people in my lifetime, and have observed, through the media, incredible acts of kindness: people jumping into rivers to save a drowning child; people emptying their bank accounts to support those in need; people taking strangers into their homes; and on and on it goes.

I confess here that I regard kindness to be a very difficult challenge. On the one hand, I consider myself, for the most part, as being a kind person – others have referred to me as such – and if I thought long and hard enough about it I could probably relate several small kindnesses I have extended to various people over the years. On the other hand, I clearly recall several unkind things I did to my mother and sister while growing up, then later on to Barbara, and to others as well. And certainly I have considerable trouble seeing myself as someone who extends unconditional kindness. I seriously question whether I could risk my own life, as other folks have done, in order to save another human being. Yes, I will frequently drop coins into the hat of a street beggar, but often I simply pass them by and then later lament my unkindness in doing so. I rationalize, as so many do, by reminding myself that I could hardly afford to support all the beggars of the world, and perhaps I am not really helping them anyway by giving in to their requests. It is a constant mind struggle. But it reinforces my opinion that my own small acts of kindness pale in comparison with major acts of kindness I have observed others perform over my years.

I think that most of us probably are emotionally and psychologically incapable of manifesting the extreme kindness extended by the relative few. However, what all of us are surely capable of is to refrain from being intentionally *unkind*. There is so much intentional unkindness in the world today (as there has been over the ages): people saying things to others to try to hurt them; people exacting revenge for a perceived slight; people damaging or stealing the property of another; people bullying others to bolster their own depleted self-image. It is rampant, to the point of teenagers taking their lives after being savaged by peers over the internet.

So here is my practical compromise, at least until I achieve a higher state of being. I have eased my doubts and reservations about my personal kindness rating by making a commitment to do my best to avoid ever again being intentionally unkind to another. I invite readers to join me in this commitment. It is a simple choice to make, carrying none of the personal risks and deprivations that accompany major acts of kindness to which I have just referred. This may be the most significant contribution each of us can make to our own inner peace, and by extension, to world peace.

I salute kindness (and the avoidance of intentional unkindness) in my short poem of the same name.

Kindness

I see random acts of kindness everywhere,
a fallen senior helped up to his feet,
handouts to the blind man on the street,
food for hungry children needing care.

I see people give their savings all to charity,
house strangers who've been forced to leave their home;
spend hours to visit folks shut in alone,
and risk their lives so others can live free.

Kindness is the end-game of respect,
humans rising over scarcity and fear,
finding strength to help a troubled peer
beyond what even sainthood might expect.

Be kind, at least be you not unkind,
to everyone with whom you chance to meet,
so ever it befalls that you must greet
death's angel, you will leave with peace of mind.

MUSIC'S GIFT

Music has been an important part of my life, but it might not have turned out that way. I recall that when I was in Grade 2, I was viciously typecast by a music teacher as a "sausage," not a "singer," and it was only through the foresight of my mother to later place me in a children's choir in Yarmouth, Nova Scotia, that I put rejection behind me. I will always be grateful to my dedicated and inspirational choir leader, Miss McKenzie, for acquainting me with music's gift.

Although my mother, an accomplished pianist, was unable to convince me to persevere with piano lessons when I was young, I took up the guitar at age 13. I started performing and writing songs, and co-founded a rock band at 15. Our band, the Asteroids, was both unsuccessful and short-lived, but astonishingly, with the passage of time, it is now recognized by rock and roll historians as one of the earliest all-Canadian bands to record a rock record in Canada, which we did in 1958. It was not a very good record, but mercifully the historians don't get into critiques. Time can be kind! The record can today be found on several compilation albums of early rock and roll, and, of course, on the internet, where almost everything can be found.

I played on and off with both a dance band and a rock band while in college, having scuttled plans I had laid out at age 17 to move to Toronto to study jazz guitar. Instead, I completed university, went to law school and started a legal career. There was a 10 year period during which I rarely touched the guitar, but Barbara must have noticed a void in my life because at age 30 she encouraged me to visit the Fredericton farmer's market one morning to meet a young U.S. "draft dodger" who was hand-crafting guitars in the backwoods of New Brunswick. I ordered one of his instruments, started playing and singing again, and my musical life opened up. I still have that guitar, part of a small collection I have accumulated over the years, and I play it often.

I studied classical guitar for a couple of years in my 30s, and even played in a music festival in Ottawa. In 1988 I recorded an album of songs "of and for the spirit," which Barbara and I had co-written, and she and I subsequently performed regularly in spiritual gatherings, choirs and ceremonies of various kinds, over many years. I still play in a swing band in Ottawa, mostly as a community service for senior citizens (like me).

One of the highlights of my musical journey was a lengthy period post-2000, during which Barbara and I joined with friends regularly to sing bluegrass/gospel music. We even occasionally performed in public venues and recording sessions. I am reminded of what has often been attributed to the venerable Pete Seeger: - If people would only sing together, the world could get along. Group singing is a warm and friendly, yet powerful, means of communication. I have watched countless "unlikely" musicians and singers step out of the closet to express themselves in this way.

That is an abbreviated snapshot of what has been a very important part of my life. While not all musical genres appeal to me – perhaps I have not learned to listen well enough - what is critical is expression and release, in whatever musical form people choose to define themselves and their cultures. I celebrate music's gift in my poem of the same name, drawing inspiration for my aging ears in quiet remembrance of Beethoven's triumph.

Music's Gift

I sometimes think how sad I'd be
were I no longer fit to hear
the rhythm and the melody
of music sounding in my ear.

Or the subtle tones of my guitar
as it vibrates in my aging hands,
the woeful wail of an old sitar,
the joyful noise of marching bands.

Music seeks an ear attuned
to the varied textures of the art,
to harmonies so deftly pruned,
to words that touch the craving heart.

Yet, though my hearing's in decline,
I reject the urge to feel denied,
recalling all those works divine
from the master, deaf to life outside.

For music would ring true inside
his head, and with a voice so clear,
he conquered senses that had died
to remain composer without peer.

Music's gift is of the mind,
and only silenced by its choice.
The song is always there to find
when we listen for its quiet voice.

SUCCESS

In November 2010 I attended the funeral of a friend who had passed away after a relatively short illness. The last time we had been together was at Christmas of the previous year, a few months before he became seriously ill. We had made it a pleasant habit over the years to get together for lunch every festive season to catch up on the prior year's activities and interests. He had recently retired, and was enjoying more time with his family than he had been able to during his busy career as a successful lawyer.

Chris had been a very good friend, colleague and supporter over many years. He encouraged me in the writing and publishing of my book *Seeing Law Differently* in 1992, and courageously (so I thought) wrote a very positive review of the book for the monthly magazine of the Canadian Bar Association. As unorthodox as the book's content was, he recommended it to many of his colleagues in the legal profession, and bought multiple copies to send to people he thought might benefit from reading what I had written. His support was extremely important to me, as I was experiencing a lot of fear and insecurity at the time about putting my spiritual viewpoint in front of the public for critical scrutiny. Chris also introduced, as prospective clients, several of his friends and acquaintances who he thought might benefit from the approach to legal challenges that I had explored in my book. He and I shared ideas about how law could and should be practiced, and in my eyes he was the embodiment of what a fine lawyer could be.

Chris was very much a family man, extremely close to his lovely wife, to his five children, whom he adored, and to his several grand-children. Our sons had been close friends, school mates and team mates in earlier years, so Chris' passing had a profound impact on all of us.

At his funeral, the large church was filled to standing-room only. I had a strong and compelling sense that everyone there felt about Chris much as I did: that he was an exceptional man who, in one way or another, had touched their lives at crucial points, as he had mine. Listening at the ceremony to recollections of his many accomplishments as a lawyer, partner, family man, scholar, athlete, poet, philosopher, neighbour and friend, I could only focus on how successful a life Chris had lived, in so many ways.

Looking back on it today, I realize that success is measured not just by *what* we do, but *how* we do it. As remarkable as Chris' many accomplishments in life and law were, what supported them, and what branded him as a truly successful man, were the more abstract, intangible, spiritual characteristics that he brought to everything he did. It is this vision of success that I have tried to capture and to honour in my short poem *Success*.

Success

It isn't wealth or fame or praise
that one's success is measured by;
or the diplomas and degrees
that line our walls before we die.
Although they mark distinct achievements
earned in striving for the best,
they're of an opaque world of form
that can obscure a truer test.

Accomplishments are ranked so highly
in a world we dream as real.
Yet the quest for recognition
often hides the fear we feel.
Basking in its tepid glow
we may doubt the price we've paid;
success may savour less than sweet,
with worry how our game's been played.

True success is measured thus,
by how a man lives out his days:
Is he in tune with higher self,
kind and caring in his ways?
Does his path embrace forgiveness,
respect for those who share his space?
If so, then at his journey's end,
success adorns his gift of grace.

MONEY

It has been quite a challenge for me to write about money. Having been raised by parents who lived through the Great Depression, I have carried throughout my life a fear of scarcity. Yet, in reviewing my years, I can now appreciate that I have always been well cared for. I have never been wealthy, by objective standards, and in some years I have made less money than in others; but almost miraculously there has always seemed to be enough coming in to provide amply for our family's needs, and to enjoy many of the pleasures that life in Canada affords. I have known many individuals and families along the way who live full and happy lives with far less income than mine. So, a rational mind would doubtless tell me that it's now time, here in my retiring years, to let go of my fear and simply trust that the Universe will provide.

I find it interesting that, in the saga of humankind, money has enjoyed such a relatively short run. First sharing, then bartering in kind, long preceded the introduction of money as a convenient means of exchange. But over that relatively short period, money has developed dominant, almost god-like, presence and influence in the day-to-day lives of so many of the world's citizens. With rapidly growing global interaction and development, its influence will spread exponentially across the entire planet.

Daily, we read in the media sordid stories of disrespect for the personal and proprietary rights of individuals, in North America and across the world. At the political level, there are dictators who horde national wealth and deprive most of their citizens of any fair share of that wealth. Vast amounts of money are used to finance wars that are, to a large extent, sparked by the misuse and coveting of wealth. On the private level, technology has opened a wide window on theft and fraud committed by highly intelligent predators. Increasing numbers of them prey on unsuspecting victims, stealing their identities in order to perpetrate crimes of enormous economic consequence for those successfully targeted. One can pay more than lip service to the age-old saying: "The love of money is the root of evil."

Yet money holds equally the promise of kindness. Many individuals who have amassed fortunes through industry, technology, sport and other forms of entertainment, have established philanthropic foundations to benefit in myriad ways those who are less fortunate. As critical as angry cynics may be of their motives, and of how socially inequitably their fortunes may have been amassed, they are nonetheless giving back. Equally, governments of wealthy nations, themselves not immune from fiscal criticism, contribute regularly in relief of disasters suffered in less fortunate nations. At ground level, many charitable organizations in Canada, among them the Canadian Red Cross (my last employer), receive millions of dollars annually from ordinary Canadians to support humanitarian causes across the world, evidencing a strong and healthy spirit of generosity in the nation.

Doubtless, money, which has no innate beauty or intrinsic value of itself, has proven to be a tremendous force for both evil and good in the world. I have chosen to allude to both in my poem *Money*, while expressing my personal faith in the inner benefits of using money in service of core lessons I espouse in this collection.

Money

The love of money, I've been told,
can be the root of evil deeds:
stealing from both young and old,
to further false, self-serving needs;
abusing power and prominence
to fatten secret bank accounts
and reinforce the dominance
of those whom God might well denounce.

The scent of money tempts the mind
with ego thoughts best laid aside,
fear of falling far behind,
of loss, of lack, of dreams denied.
As envy taints one's sense of worth
and challenges integrity,
desire can slowly foster birth
of a soul devoid of honesty.

And yet, this scene need not be so,
when fear gives way to confidence.
A kinder vision starts to grow,
restoring faith in providence.
For it's not how much one has that counts,
but rather what one puts it to.
A Voice invites us to renounce
the selfish uses we pursue.

Money hath no innate beauty,
nor value on the other side,
save peace to those whose inner duty
insists it not be misapplied.
The joy of money comes from sharing,
whatever be the time or place,
random acts of love and caring
give it thus a human face.

EVERYMAN

I have long been of the view that we human beings all harbour an infinite range of thoughts, some beautiful, and some vicious. I refer to "thoughts," as opposed to factors that shape intelligence, competence and individuality. Essentially, I am speaking of thoughts that surround our interactions with others, whether human or animal. I am not suggesting that we all ponder committing atrocities such as murder, child molestation, kidnapping and torture; but we are all aware that such thoughts do exist within the inventories of our minds, even though they will seem repulsive to most of us. And although an ultimate goal may be to hold in mind only loving thoughts towards others, few will reach that pinnacle. In all honesty, it is very difficult, if not impossible, to banish every dark thought from our conscious and unconscious minds.

Speaking personally, I am well aware of some hurtful thoughts that have crossed my mind over my lifetime, a few of which, I must confess, I have acted upon, much to my regret and embarrassment. However, for the most part I have been able to pass over such thoughts, so as not to manifest them in behaviours that could be injurious to others or to myself. At the same time, I can credit myself with carrying through with many beautiful thoughts that have brought rewards to others and to me. I believe that the same can be said of most of us.

It is often said in "new age" circles that "we are one," and I believe that there are various meanings that can be attributed to that affirmation, and various ways it can be understood. My own take on it is that there is a linking of minds, and a resulting collectivity of thought, that warrants careful self-scrutiny before jumping to judgment of another, or of his or her conduct. The oft-heard saying "There, but for the grace of God, go I" holds considerable truth for me. But for different, and ostensibly better, choices among the thoughts that inhabit my mind, I might find myself in situations that attract condemnation by society, to say nothing of self-contempt. As well, cultural, historic, social, economic and political circumstances can influence us to make choices that may seem bizarre and wrong from others' limited, more comfortable, vantage points, but in context could well be decisions they too might make.

I sometimes ask myself, "Who am I?" and what is it that makes me, deep down, a different person than anyone else? In God's eyes we may all be perfect, but I have come to accept that it is the choices we make to act, or not to act, upon the thoughts we hold that tell the story: – are we kind or unkind? Do we treat others with respect (to pick up on themes of this collection)? It is these choices and decisions that determine who we are. It follows from this belief that people *can* change, for the better or for the worse, because they can always make different, and hopefully better, choices and decisions than ones they have made before. I have tried to capture the essence of this thinking in my short poem *Everyman*, which follows.

Everyman

He is my neighbour, Everyman,
his mind harbouring myriad thoughts
of light and darkness;
thoughts both kind and unkind,
respectful and disrespectful,
salutary and hurtful,
selfless and selfish,
thoughts of life and of death.

I too am Everyman,
for across my mind pass
the very thoughts for which
I laud and accuse my neighbour,
thoughts majestic and depraved,
enlightened and earthbound,
ever causing me to question
the "me" of who I am.

Though each of us is Everyman,
the "me" my neighbour greets
embodies what I've chosen
from the mindscape of consciousness.
The manifestation of thoughts,
choosing what I say and do,
transforms Everyman
into the person I've become.

GRATITUDE

This is a "warm and fuzzy" theme, reprising advice handed down over the centuries, heralded in prose, poetry and song. I recall from years ago Bing Crosby's hit recording *Count Your Blessings*, a highly inspirational song that reached the top of the charts. It is always a blessing when popular songs with such a positive message achieve commercial success. It seems to occur less frequently today, but still happens from time to time. Josh Groban's hit *You Raise Me Up* is one of several relatively recent examples of inspirational pop that generated wide popular success.

The practice of gratitude sounds easy to do, yet can be difficult to accomplish. It is far too easy for any of us to slip into the grip of fear, to become consumed by anger, resentment, envy or feelings of being unfairly treated. These negative emotions and feelings can block our willingness to look on the bright side of situations, to find the "silver lining," as is said. And it cannot be overlooked that for much of the world's population, blessings in the midst of life's bitter challenges may seem hard to find. Those who lack health, wealth, food, clothing, medical treatment and other basics in the inventory of the more fortunate, those who are beset by war or famine, and those eking out an existence in poverty-stricken third world countries, may have to look far deeper than I do for things to be grateful for. Yet it is equally important for all of us to make the same effort, if we are to find happiness in whatever social and economic environment we inhabit. I'm certain that we all know of well-off people in affluent North American communities who live unhappy lives, even though, by all objective standards, they appear to have so much to be grateful for. I venture to say that most of the world's population would gladly trade places with them.

It is frequently said that gratitude is an "attitude," and one that we can choose to adopt, or choose not to. I believe that to be a true observation. Attitude is shaped and developed through choice and practice. It is fully complementary to and supportive of the "kind and respectful" attitude I have put forward in this collection as being vital to a civilized society, and to personal fulfilment. When practiced regularly, gratitude can richly enhance the quality of life, as we experience it.

For those of you who may stumble over my reference to "my Larrivée" in my short poem *Gratitude*, which follows, it refers to my rosewood acoustic steel-string guitar, which I purchased several years ago. For it, and for the other guitars in my modest collection, dating back almost 40 years, I remain immensely grateful.

Gratitude

Whenever I'm inclined to fear
that darkness lurks outside my door,
I offer thanks that I am here,
and think of all I'm grateful for.

A cooling swim on a summer day,
a freshening breeze as the sun slips away.
Moments to glide on an old wooden swing,
hearing a church bell's evening ring.

A good night's sleep on a comfy bed,
in a quiet room with a roof o'erhead,
the angel who became my bride
still resting, breathing, by my side.

The clothes I wear, the food I eat,
the steps I take with aging feet.
Friends and family with whom to share
a glass, a meal, a song, a prayer.

Melodies sung in harmony
to the gentle tones of my Larrivée.
Country tunes from long ago
recounting tales of love and woe.

Simple blessings do abound
whene'er we stop to look around.
To come to know beatitude,
we need but practice gratitude.

THE WITNESS

Over the years I have been fascinated by the relationship between truth and justice, particularly in the area of penal law. Frequently I hear or read about what seem to be bizarre charges, convictions and acquittals, and I tell myself that there must be more to the story than appears. Our vision of justice is broadly premised on the assumption that out of a judicial trial will emerge the truth. And yet it strikes me that "truth" is an elusive and illusory concept, and that to deal with situations of societal discord on the basis of guilt or innocence, and then base the verdict on this rather limiting criterion of truth, is hardly the vision of justice I would hold for an ideal society.

While that brief critique reflects on my part a gross oversimplification of a complex process, few would disagree that truth is a driving force within our system of justice. Almost a cliché, it is often said that the adversary system is the greatest invention for the discovery of truth. Cross-examination by skilled lawyers will attempt to "out" lies and misperceptions, throwing into question the truth of the witness' story (if successful), or else reinforcing its truth (if unsuccessful).

Speaking personally, I think I might have a hard time testifying as a witness at a criminal trial. The oath, which requires me to tell the truth, the whole truth and nothing but the truth, would be my first challenge. I have come to accept that my own perceptions of reality do not entirely, if at all, represent "truth." They are highly influenced by my fears, hopes, biases, past recollections, cultural leanings, education, and so on. "Projection makes perception," as the idea is sometimes put. Essentially, it means that I see what I want to see: i.e. I project thoughts that colour what I seem to perceive. Also, my physical limitations, such as eyesight and hearing, may distort what I think I saw and heard. Another concern is that the legal rules of evidence filter out much of what I might say about the larger context of an event. They are designed in large part to reduce the amount of inaccurate information that is presented to the court, and to a lesser degree to narrow the scope of the inquiry. These evidence rules filter out facts and considerations that might give deeper insight into an event. In fairness, some of this evidence is admissible in sentencing proceedings, after an accused has been found guilty, but at that later stage it does not undermine the "truth" on which the guilt of the accused has been decided.

While I can accept that the underlying purpose of the oath is to commit witnesses to be honest in what they say, and not to lie or edit their testimony, the language of truth, and the institutional assumptions about truth, have contributed, in my view, to documented injustices. Innocent persons have been accused of offences, convicted and imprisoned, or otherwise penalized, for conduct that, if the full context were known, might elicit a more compassionate response in a different forum of accountability. Conversely, guilty persons have been unjustly set free. I do recognize that the multitude of offences that have been promulgated by law makers, and the sheer volume of charges laid daily by law enforcement officials, leave little desk or court time available for situations to be as thoroughly explored and resolved as advocates of restorative justice might choose to see. Still, through my poem *The Witness*, I express the hope that our society can move beyond plaudits over the excellence of our system of justice, and eventually embrace a more compassionate approach to dealing with disrespectful behaviour.

The Witness

I know not truth! The witness cried,
and cannot swear that I will tell
the whole truth, nothing but the truth,
else find myself consigned to hell.
For what my eyes recall they've seen,
and what my brain has deigned to keep,
cut but a short and shallow seam
in a story that runs deep.

Ask not for truth! Oh learned judge,
it's not there for me to see;
simply ask what I believe,
that I say it honestly.
I'll find the words, as best I can,
that, recounting thus a fuller tale,
might salvage yet a worthy man
whose fate weighs in the scale.

Truth lies beyond these human eyes,
e'er shadowed as they be;
where justice courts illusion
it will earn no dignity.
Let not Justitia reign with truth,
as has been her fashion,
entreat her to be less aloof
to the justice of compassion.

WORRY

I confess that I have always been a bit of a worrier! When I was in high school, and in university, I worried unduly about exams, to the point that it began to take its toll on me physically. I would regularly suffer through weeks of spastic bowel syndrome, until the results were released and I discovered that there had been nothing at all to worry about – I did just fine! So eventually I made the decision that I was not going to live that way any longer. Through conscious effort and practice I was able to will myself from under the grip of that chronic and painful syndrome.

Although not to the degree that had brought on ill health, I continued my pattern of worrying. I worried about our children; about family finances; about job performance; about the state of my vehicles, about the future; and on and on I could go. Most of what I worried about I had little or no control over. Rationally I understood that, but emotionally it was a different story.

I have come to accept, over the years, that there was, and is, nothing exceptional about my pattern. I dare say that worrying is a common activity for millions of Canadians, and for hundreds of millions of people around the world. It seems that the greater one's sense of responsibility, the more worrying one does. Yet medical research has established how detrimental it can be to health, even if the symptoms are not as apparent as mine were in my early years. Unproductive as it is, worrying erodes our energy, resources, health, happiness and peace of mind, with no corresponding benefit. How helpful it would be to erase worry from our repertoire of fear!

That is not to say that we should go about our lives with reckless abandon. The "good" cousin of worry is *caution*. If, as I suggest in my poem, worry is the "handmaiden of fear," then caution might well be characterized as *the executor of discerning*. Discernment is a rational trait, necessary to make sound decisions in life. Most of us would agree that it makes sense to take steps to prevent our children from playing on busy streets, which is the exercise of *caution*; but, having taken those cautionary steps, it makes little or no sense to *worry* that they may circumvent them and be run over by an oncoming car. There are many people who believe, with evidence in support, that worrying can attain such a focus as to manifest the very thing that one is worrying about. Our thoughts can be that powerful!

Much has been written in self-help manuals to assist us to eliminate, or at least control, our tendency to worry. I recall one writer advocating that people might consider allocating a small time slot each day in which to do all their worrying, and then leave the rest of the day worry-free – *i.e.* "parking" their worries for scheduled attention, so to speak. Others have promoted the value of combating worry through strong religious faith or spiritual belief. Needless to say, I applaud anyone who can maintain confidence that their God or the Universe will protect and provide, for they are avoiding, or at least reducing, the grim toll that worrying exacts.

I wrote the short poem *Worry* as an antidote to the stress I could feel building up inside me as I watched global economic uncertainty unfold in 2011, with its attendant market volatility. Sensing it as a potential threat to the sustainability of my retirement plans, I felt in dire need of an affirmation that might help kindle the healing forces of hope and trust.

Worry

Worry, take leave!
You are hardly a friend;
you ask me to grieve
'fore the scene's at an end.

Handmaiden of fear,
misuser of mind,
don't dare to draw near,
for I've left you behind.

What's happened is done,
and can't be replayed;
but my future is one
that has yet to be made.

So I'll let it unfold,
and live for right now;
I'll resist growing old
with a stern, wrinkled brow.

Worry, be gone!
For your vision, so glum,
falls shy of the dawn
of my days still to come.

GODLIGHT

I have alluded previously in this collection to my belief that there resides, within the mind of everyone, a metaphorical spark of goodness, or "Godness," which is an inherent sense or remembrance of God's pure and perfect Consciousness. When sustained, the spark ignites, glows and evolves into what I call here "Godlight." My life in this worldly consciousness provides countless opportunities for me to sustain the spark. Equally, it provides me with opportunities to dampen the spark, and to retard it from igniting and glowing.

In my understanding, God is not an anthropomorphic deity with a master plan for me and for the world. God is personal to me in the sense that this tiny spark of goodness, offering me the experience of Godlight, is embedded within me. Although it is impossible for any of us, in this human dimension, to permanently dismantle our egos, the closer we can come to doing so the closer we come to escaping the pleasure/pain cycle that dominates the lives of most of us here on the planet. It is this cycle that brings on much of the despair, unhappiness, violence and ill health we witness and experience.

I believe that we sustain the spark by practicing respect for ourselves and others, kindness to all, compassion, honesty, non-judgment and forgiveness, by letting go of ego choices and, ultimately, by nurturing a peaceful state. While it would be enormously difficult for anyone in this world to embrace this state in every situation, around the clock every day, my goal at this late stage of my life is to avoid dampening the spark as much as I can, and to sustain it as consistently as I can, as I go about my daily routine.

While it is accepted in medical circles that in most cases the body heals itself, I have come to believe that self-healing is accelerated by focusing upon the radiance of Godlight within me, and by feeling its energy flow through me to bring health and healing to my mind and body. When my health starts to break down, I attribute it to choices I have made that are not in tune with Godlight (which I have referred to as "dampening the spark"). Yet, through meditative recognition and acceptance of Godlight, and with a renewed commitment to sustain the spark by letting go of fear and releasing the unforgiving thoughts and judgments that eat away at my mind, body and soul, I can feel health returning.

While I have practiced this meditation on many occasions to overcome what seemed to be the onset of illness, I cannot claim that it holds out any vain promise of immortality, for we all pass on; our bodies die. Nor would I deny that there are many health conditions that require medical intervention. Nonetheless, I am confident that by embracing my belief in Godlight I can enhance my stay here, and eventually support a peaceful transition to whatever consciousness lies beyond.

I have tried to capture the gist of my meditation in the final poem of this collection, which follows.

Godlight

I welcome the radiant glow of Godlight,
dawning from the tiny spark of goodness
that I sustain within me.
I am grateful for the gift
of health and healing that it brings,
e'er I awaken to receive it.

Here, in silent meditation,
I feel its energy flow through me.
I sense healing take form,
refreshing my mind,
renewing my body,
restoring my soul.

AND TO CONCLUDE . . .

So, where am I now, more than a year after beginning this retirement project? What, if anything, has writing this collection accomplished? Is there any real importance attached to the pursuit of love, kindness, respect and other core lessons I have celebrated in my writing, or is it a silly, idealistic notion that is impossible to carry out in this world and makes no tangible difference to the human condition? As those are questions I have asked myself, I choose to conclude by sharing some brief final thoughts with readers.

One might think that if everyone in the world were to follow this path, we could achieve world peace. We could, but of course that is hardly realistic. The carnage and atrocities that so many people of the world continue to commit against others, the anarchistic, senseless citizen riots in Vancouver and in the United Kingdom in the summer of 2011, and other destructive examples too numerous to detail, reflect the disrespect for person and property that is rampant in today's world. It seems easier for people to embrace fear, in its many manifestations – insecurity, anger, greed, hostility, insult, hatred, attack – than it is to embrace love. We human beings seem to exhibit a strange and strong resistance to love and its practices. Not only is broad adherence to the path I describe a pipe dream; even if it were possible followers would doubtless have differing interpretations of its requirements. I can see that there would always be conflict, though perhaps less violent than what the world currently experiences.

So, my message is not about world peace in any macro sense. That said, I do believe that each loving act of kindness and respect eliminates or avoids a potential conflict or hurt, and in that way incrementally diminishes universal unrest. At the micro level, I believe that there is a tiny contribution toward peace in the world that can be attributed to each loving act we carry out, imperceptible though that contribution might seem in global terms.

More notably, I believe that there is a rich personal benefit for everyone who chooses to practice these lessons, and for those with whom they interact. I can feel the benefit inside myself, and I can sense it in people I relate to. Intangible as it is, I cannot describe the experience any more definitively than I have done already in my writing. Because composing these poems and musings has required me to look at myself and my surroundings more critically than I had ever done before, it has widened my eyes to what I feel is a greater understanding of ideas I might once have glossed over as being pretty airy. The path I have chosen in my remaining years is of utmost importance to completing my life's journey with a sense of purpose. Such is the cycle of life, that what may have seemed far less compelling earlier on, we come to value later in life.

In saying that, it is important to express my hope that kindness, respect and other loving acts are not reserved for days when we can enjoy the late winter sun. I believe that they are compatible with any journey through life, at any stage. They will pay dividends even for those who, more than I, cherish the excitement, thrills, risks and adventure of mainstream paths in today's world, now so widely accessible through modern invention, innovation and technology. Inner peace, and a sense of self worth and the worth of others, are valued states on whatever path one follows in the world, whatever one's goals may be. I am convinced that they are crucial ingredients in life's recipe for success and happiness.

DEDICATION

I have chosen to dedicate this collection of poems and musings jointly to my wife Barbara, and to the memory of her mother, Leva Matchett.

The first poem I ever wrote, many years ago (with the exception of a horrendous poem I composed as an English assignment in my first year at university), was a tribute to Barbara's mother, a woman who not only wrote charming poetry herself, but had a deep appreciation of poetry and a spell-binding way of reciting long narrative poems. She brought poetry to life through her delivery. Even though she had lost her sight many years before, she retained in memory what she had absorbed in her earlier years. Yours truly (who, as a student, had seemed incapable of memorizing two consecutive lines of poetry, and who, as a singer-songwriter has difficulty remembering the words to songs, even those I have written myself) was truly mesmerized by the easy flow of words coming from this woman's lips.

Poetry is more than an art form; a poem can carry values through the ages, and expressions of deep thought, succinctly and inspirationally. Listening to this woman recite opened my eyes and ears to the gift she had nurtured and shared so lovingly and respectfully throughout her lifetime.

The poem that follows, *The Gift*, was a present I gave to Barbara shortly after it was composed in 1983. I have overheard her on several occasions tell friends that it remains one of her more trea-sured gifts - perhaps because it was so unexpected of me to write a poem for her. We included the poem within a newsletter Barbara and I co-published in years past, to accompany a memorial Barbara wrote for her mother shortly after her death in 1994. Apart from a few minor edits that I have made recently, the poem reads as it did originally in 1983.

Barbara's mother never read this poem, and may not even have appreciated it as a *poem*. In her universe, poetry was about rhythm and rhyme. Blank and free verse likely would not have moved her much. Nonetheless, I'm certain she would have appreciated the thought that underlies the words.

The Gift

Unlike the old woman who lived in a shoe,
she knew exactly what to do
for her children.
Acquaint them with the beauty of a poem and, through this,
instill in them a sense of dedication
to virtues like honesty, love and trust,
which we must, if we are to survive our ordeals,
strive to live by.

There is an inner beauty to this woman
that radiates when she recites her lines,
lines taught to her by her mother,
lines spoken to be passed through generations
lest we should forget the joys and frustrations
of those who came before us,
or fail to understand the values
that helped them cope with another age.

Her memory gives vision to eyes that have failed,
and the words come clearly and confidently,
as if, only yesterday, her mother, dead now for almost forty years,
had sat her down to introduce her to the people living in the lines
that have long since become a part of her.
As she recites, there is a quiet reverence,
a sense of awe and admiration, a concentration not inspired
by the electronic gadgets that amuse today's generation.

As I watch my wife, her youngest daughter,
spellbound by the words that flow so simply from her mother's lips,
words not heard perhaps for twenty years,
or however long it may have been since, as a young girl,
she left her mother's home to make her way in life,
I sense that something has been given
whose content I had not before understood,
whose worth is incalculable, whose span is forever.

As for Barbara, I will only add to what I have already shared in this collection that she has taught me much in the half century or so that we have been together, supporting me through good times and in the face of challenges. In honour of her 70th birthday, in the autumn of 2011, I wrote these verses for her, which I am happy to share with readers as my closing poem.

Barbara's Birthday - 2011

In this cosmic dream of time we count the years,
as if they were the measure of our lives;
yet, no matter how intently mind contrives,
nothing is, in truth, as it appears.

Although your outward features gently change,
as we see each summer season come and go,
remaining constant are your inner glow,
and your values, which time cannot rearrange.

Like the river waters flowing past your window,
winding 'round each richly wooded bend,
your love has no beginning, and no ending,
nurturing all in need of it to grow.

So thank you for the spirit who you are,
for the song you bring to everything you do;
I am drawn to the Light that e'er surrounds you,
as if you were a brightly shining star.

Although we're counting three score years and ten,
illusion doesn't blind me to the truth;
for your timeless beauty offers certain proof
that we'll share this happy moment yet again.

CPSIA information can be obtained at www.ICGtesting.com
Printed in the USA
LVOW100848101012

302167LV00001B/9/P